The Unique Candlewicking Collection

v

The Unique Candlewicking Collection

Jan Potter

SALLY MILNER PUBLISHING

DEDICATION

To my three talented daughters, Lynda, Heather and
Karen, thank you for the enjoyment your love and
friendship has been to me.

First published in 2000 by
Sally Milner Publishing Pty Ltd
PO Box 2104
Bowral NSW 2576
Australia

© Jan Potter 2000

Design by Anna Warren, Warren Ventures P/L
Photography by Sergio Santos
Back cover photograph by Heather Evans
Editing by Lyneve Rappell
Printed in Hong Kong

National Library of Australia
Cataloguing in Publication Data

Potter, Jan (Jan Heather)
    The unique candlewicking collection

    ISBN 1 86351 269 1.

    1. Candlewicking (Embroidery). I. Title. (Series : Milner craft series)

    746.44

Disclaimer
The information in this instruction book is presented in good faith.
However, no warranty is given, nor results guaranteed, nor is freedom from
any patent to be inferred. Since we have no control over the use of
information contained in this book, the publisher and the author disclaim
liability for untoward results.

The Stitcher

Who's that stitching by the window,
Absorbed in placing every stitch with care?
Oblivious to all around her,
Lost in dreams creation brings.
Occasional glances out the window,
Resting eyes on distant scenes of trees and skies,
Recalled by flashing needle, threads and canvas.
Art in progress—needle painted.

JAN POTTER

CONTENTS

ACKNOWLEDGMENTS

The excitement of writing a first book cannot be dulled. I feel honoured that *Wild Flowers in Candlewicking* is as popular as ever.

I'd like to thank all of you who have bought or borrowed it and enjoyed making the projects, I know you will enjoy my new book. To my mothers for loving everything I did; my daughters who were always interested, also my wonderful and most encouraging friends, Liz and Shirley. We were all chafing at the bit well before the book was finished.

To my publishers, Libby and Ian, for being so enthusiastic and helpful; Jenny, who gave me lots of helpful quilting hints; Annie Lane Designs for their lovely ceramic and terracotta cat buttons. To all those understanding and encouraging people at work who were interested in the book's progress. And to all of those unnamed others, realising it or not, who have been supportive in the creation of another book.

Thanks to all of you.

INTRODUCTION

A second book? Well, it was always in the back of my mind and I figured that if I could do it once, why not twice or more?

Candlewicking is one of the easiest of embroideries, requiring only a few simple stitches to create an elegant piece that melds with most decors in any room of the house. I have included projects for both beginners and experienced needleworkers, although no design is harder than another—it just takes a little more time to complete. The time spent, however, is well worthwhile.

Candlewicking has a long and close association with quilting. An appreciation of mini-patchwork quilts prompted me to include some basic information on quilting for those of you who, like me, wish to combine a little of the two arts.

The projects have been embroidered traditionally in cream on cream and in a modern coloured version so both the effects can be appreciated side by side.

Now it's ready for you all out there in the world of stitches and thread to let me know what you think of it.

Enjoy it, as I have enjoyed preparing it for you, a smorgasbord of unique designs and ideas.

Start wherever you like, make it into whatever appeals to you; do it coloured, do it cream, do it white, do it with a friend or do it alone, only relish it!

MATERIALS & EQUIPMENT

FABRICS

Traditionally calico or homespun have been used with candlewicking embroidery, but that was when nothing else was available. Today we have such a wide range of beautiful fabrics, so let's experiment and be creative.

This book shows you examples with voile, linen (old & new), homespun, hemp, waffle cloth, wool and even drop shadow satin. Some of these are easier to work than others and maybe a beginner would find the homespun the best to work on at first.

I know that will throw out a challenge to those of you who feel you can do just as well first go on satin. Well, good for you! Give it a go and don't let anything stop you!

THREADS

As with fabrics the choice of threads these days is as wide or as narrow as you allow it. For that beautiful and elegant cream-on-cream or white-on-white there are threads such as those from **Sullivans**, **Habycrafts** and **Cascade House Australia** who all have lovely creams and whites. I found Cascade House yarn very smooth and easy to use. They have a small range of country colours also.

Other threads I have used are: **Panda™ Regal 4-ply Knitting & Crochet Cotton**, **DMC Perle** no. 5 & 8, and **DMC Traditions**. These threads come in a range of colours—plain and shaded—as well as the neutrals, and are well worth using. Some companies are specially overdying the perle threads, and just seeing them sparks ideas of ways in which they can be used.

EdMar Rayon Threads from Ristel Threads are another lovely group of threads more commonly used for Brazilian embroidery. These add beautiful sheen to the work and come in lots of colours. Many of them are shaded in two, three or more colours; so one thread will give you a whole range of colour. Like all threads, variegated threads can be slightly different from one dye lot to the next, so buy all the thread you will need for a project at one time. Take care to keep this thread untangled and it will give your project a beautiful finish.

DMC Medici Wool is a fine wool thread and absolutely lovely on woollen fabric. It comes in a variety of colours to suit any mood, as well as natural and white. Try it on the baby blanket for a new child or grandchild.

Chenille Craftworks is an acrylic yarn I found on a fossicking trip one day. It made the colonial knots on the baby blanket look fantastic. Work with a huge needle, like the type used for sewing knitted garments together. That type of needle has a large eye, which makes a big enough hole to pull the thread through without it bunching.

DMC Metallic Perle no. 5—along with the antique gold and pearl beads—gave the Christmas decorations an extra sparkle. Other nice touches are the use of silk and organza ribbons, little brass findings and ceramic buttons (for which I thank Annie Lane Designs).

When working with all threads, keep them untangled by letting the needle dangle and the thread spin out, when you see them starting to twist. A thread as long as your arm is a good manageable size to work with.

NEEDLES

For me, the best needle is the one I can see to thread! Of course, if the thread being used is fine, then use a smaller needle. Conversely, if the thread is thicker, use a needle with a larger eye.

On the whole, I use Crewel needles (average size no. 7–11) for candlewicking because the eye is a little larger and longer. The main reason for having a larger eye is that it seems to stop the thread wearing as much at the eye as it is pulled through the fabric. For that reason, it's easiest to work with a thread about as long as your arm.

EMBROIDERY HOOPS

I find these useful for keeping the fabric at a good tension. A frame in a stand is helpful, in that you have both hands free to work. Most of the work in this book was completed on a 4" (10 cm) or 5" (13 cm) hoop. It may be advisable—for the small embroideries—to cut the fabric to size *after* the embroidery is completed.

TECHNIQUES

TRANSFERRING DESIGNS TO FABRIC

1. Set up a light box. If you don't have a real one, you can use either a window or a glass table with a light underneath.

2. Fold your fabric to find the centre and squeeze a crease in it.

3. Trace the design onto tissue paper.

4. Find the centre of the design by ruling a box close around the design and then ruling diagonals. Where the diagonals cross is the centre of the design.

5. Tape the design to the light table then centre the fabric and tape it to the light box as well. Turn on the light and trace the design with a pencil.

6. If the fabric is hard to see through, lay the fabric onto the light table first, then place a sheet of graphite carbon (as used for folk art) on top and tape or pin it to the fabric. Place the design on top and use an empty biro or stylus to trace over the design.

7. **Make sure** the design is centred, and that the edges of the design and the fabric are parallel.

TO MITRE CORNERS

1. Fold the edge of the fabric down ³⁄₁₆" (5 mm), turn under and press. Fold a ¾" (2 cm) main hem and

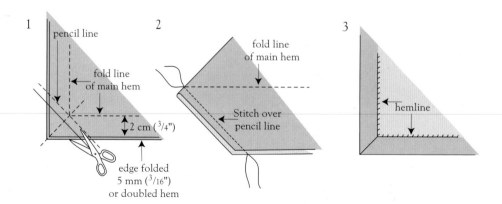

press. Unfold the hem once and draw a diagonal line on the wrong side at the point of the hemline. Cut off the corner leaving a ⁵⁄₁₆" (5 mm) seam allowance.

2. Fold back the corner with the right sides together, and pin and stitch along the marked diagonal line.

3. Turn the corner right side out, and press. Finish the hem with blind hem stitching.

MAKING TWISTED CORD

1. Tie the ends of the thread together to make one huge loop. Hold the knot in one hand.

2. Fold the loop so that there are two loops together for a twist that is four threads thick.

3. Put one or two fingers through the loop, at one end.

4. Holding the threads taut, twist the loop keeping the knot at the end. (It won't move much after the first few twists.) The cord is twisted enough when it becomes tight on your fingers.

5. Take hold of the centre of the twist (either hold it lightly between your lips or have someone else hold it for you).

6. Slacken the cord, gradually letting it twist on itself. (It automatically twists and won't unravel if you let go.) If the twist bubbles a bit, put your finger in the bottom and pull to even it out, while holding the two ends together.

7. To make a particular length of cord, measure the thread to approximately ten times the length you want the finished cord to be.

TEA DYED FABRIC

1. In a bowl, make a strong brew of five or six tea bags in 4 cups (1 litre) of boiling water.

2. Let it steep for at least 20 minutes.

3. Fold the fabric into a manageable square, then tightly fan fold (or concertina) the square to give a streaky finish.

4. Dip the fabric into the tea and hold it under about 20 minutes (or longer if you desire a darker colour).

5. Squeeze the tea out of the fabric and rinse it slightly before unfolding.

6. Hang the fabric to dry outside, because the fabric will darken a little in sunlight.

QUILTING

Complete the embroidery, and wash the piece by hand to freshen it up and remove any pattern marks. Wring out the piece in a towel and dry. Starch before drying or spray starch and iron on the back.

1. Cut the calico backing and wadding to the same size as the embroidered front.

2. Sandwich the wadding between the embroidered front and the calico backing.

3. Pin the three layers together, flattening out any puckers.

4. Tack in rows—no more than 1" (2.5 cm) apart—along the grain of the fabric.

5. A frame or a hoop can be used to hold the quilting, if you like, but a small piece is easily held in the hands once it is tacked together.

6. Quilting stitches are best kept quite small—about 7 to 10 stitches to 1" (2.5 cm).

7. Use a single strand of quilting cotton (such as Gütermann 100% quilting cotton) with cotton fabric, because quilting thread is stronger than ordinary machine thread.

8. Begin quilting by poking the needle straight through the layers of fabric from the back to the front. A small distance away, push the needle through—this time from the front to the back—to complete one stitch.

9. Continue following the individual directions for each piece.

BINDING THE QUILTS

1. After the quilting is completed, overlock or zigzag all the sides together.

2. Pin the binding to the right side of two opposite

sides of the quilt. Machine stitch the binding carefully in place, keeping an even distance from the embroidered border line.

3. Turn the binding to the back. Double over a hem on the binding, and turn in the ends. Pin the binding from the front to hold the hem in place.

4. Hand stitch the hem in place at the back of the quilt, or position your sewing machine needle 'in the ditch' on the front, as close as possible to the binding, and sew the binding in place.

5. Sew the other two sides in the same fashion to complete the quilt.

FINISHING THE BANNERS

1. After the quilting is finished, overlock or zigzag the edges of the layers together, ¾" (2 cm) from the edge of the border.

2. Pin the piping to the edge, starting at the bottom point.

3. Machine sew next to the outer row of stem stitch.

3. Pin the edge flat to the back, and stitch it down.

4. Pin the outer backing fabric to the back (inside the cord), turning in a small hem as you go. Hem stitch the outer backing in place.

HANGING THE QUILTS & BANNERS

1. Measure a suitable piece of dowelling, and paint it to suit your work—if you wish.

2. Sew velcro patches along the top back of the piece.

3. Glue the corresponding velcro patches to the dowelling.

4. Attach a cord to the dowelling, and then secure the piece to the dowelling by the velcro.

CARE OF THE PIECES

Washing

This embroidery is easily hand washed; so don't be afraid to do it. Use wool wash for woollens and Lux Flakes™ for linens and polyester such as the drop shadow satin. Homespun and calico respond well to plain laundry detergent. If there is a stubborn mark, try a bit of Sard Wonder™ soap on the spot.

Ironing

Always iron the pieces on the wrong side of the fabric, with a folded towel underneath. This keeps the embroidery in relief instead of squashed flat and sitting awkwardly. Make sure the iron is not too hot for the fabric. If you are not sure what temperature is suitable for your fabric, check by ironing a scrap of fabric first.

THE PROJECTS

_enlarge to
135% on a
photocopier_

Wattle Border Table Mat
CREAM ON CREAM

Fabric

Linen: 15¾" x 9" (40 cm x 23 cm).

Thread

DMC Perle no. 8 (ecru.)

Procedure

1. Transfer the Wattle Border design to the centre of
    the linen (see Techniques).

2. Stitch the design as follows:
    - *leaves, satin stitch*
    - *wattle, colonial knots*
    - *stem, stem stitch.*

3. Finish the Table Mat with mitred corners (see
    Techniques) using a ¾" (2 cm) hem on the front side
    of the fabric.

4. Work two rows of coral stitch along the hem.

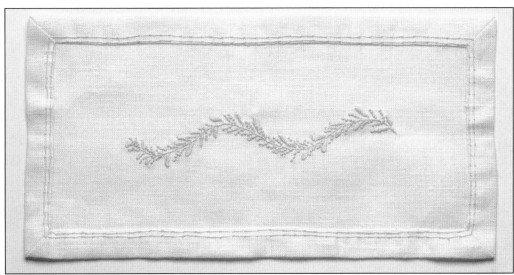

Gumleaf Table Runner
CREAM ON CREAM

Fabric

Linen: 35" x 22" (89 cm x 56 cm).

Thread

Panda ™ Regal 2-ply Knitting and Crotchet Cotton (ecru), or DMC Perle no. 8 (ecru).

Procedure

1. Transfer the Gumleaf Border design onto each end of the linen runner (see Techniques).

2. Stitch the design as follows:
    * *leaves, continuous fly stitch*
    * *stems, colonial knots, worked closely*
    * *nuts, round part in satin stitch, flared part in buttonhole stitch.*

3. When the embroidery is finished, turn a ¼" (0.5 cm) hem—either to the front or the back— on each edge of the linen. Turn the hem the same width again, and stitch a blind hem finish.

enlarge to 135% on a photocopier

Antique Flower Plate Doily
CREAM ON CREAM

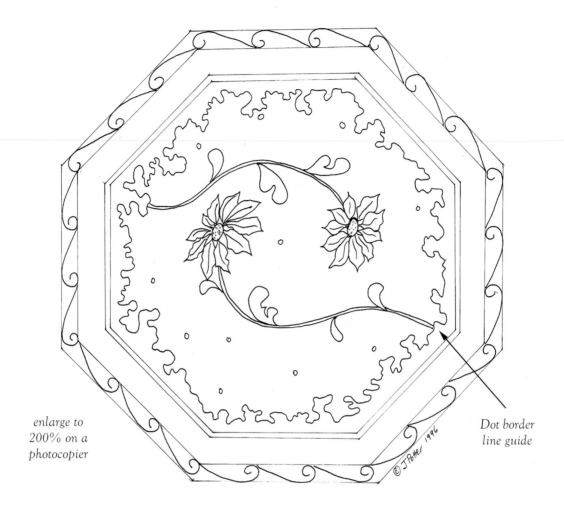

*enlarge to
200% on a
photocopier*

© J Potter 1996

*Dot border
line guide*

Materials

Linen: 10" sq (26 cm sq).

Threads

Sullivans Candlewicking Cotton (40251 natural).

Procedure

1. Transfer the Antique Flower Plate design onto the
    fabric (see Techniques for instructions).

2. Stitch the design as follows:
    * *flowers, continuous fly stitch*
    * *flower centres, close colonial knots, single thread*

- *stems, double row of stem stitch*
- *leaves, satin stitch*
- *dots inside the irregular line, spaced colonial knots, double thread*
- *edges and waves, stem stitch.*

3. When the embroidery is finished, turn the hems ½" (1 cm) to either the front or the back. Turn again the same width, and stitch with a blind hem finish.

Voile Table Topper

PALE BLUE ON WHITE

Materials

Voile (or your choice): 36" sq (1 m sq.)

Threads

DMC Perle no. 8 (775 pale blue).

Sullivans Candlewicking Cotton (natural 40251).

Procedure

enlarge both designs to 200% on a photocopier

1. Transfer the Bridal Veil Clematis Basket design to the centre of the voile and the Large Bridal Veil Clematis design the corners (see Techniques).

2. Stitch the designs as follows:

Corner designs
- *all leaves, flowers and dead heads, stem stitch (775 pale blue)*
- *centre stamens, pistil stitch (775 pale blue)*
- *random dots, colonial knots (775 pale blue)*

Centre design
- *basket, stem stitch (Sullivans natural)*
- *flowers, detached chain stitch with colonial knot centre (775 pale blue)*

• *tendrils, stem stitch with colonial knot at end (775 pale blue)*

• *random colonial knots in blue, scattered all over as work is in progress.*

3. If you wish, mitre the corners. Otherwise, blind hem stitch or machine stitch a 1" (2.5 cm) double hem all around.

4. Using Perle no. 8 (775 pale blue), stem stitch over the hem line on the right side of the fabric.

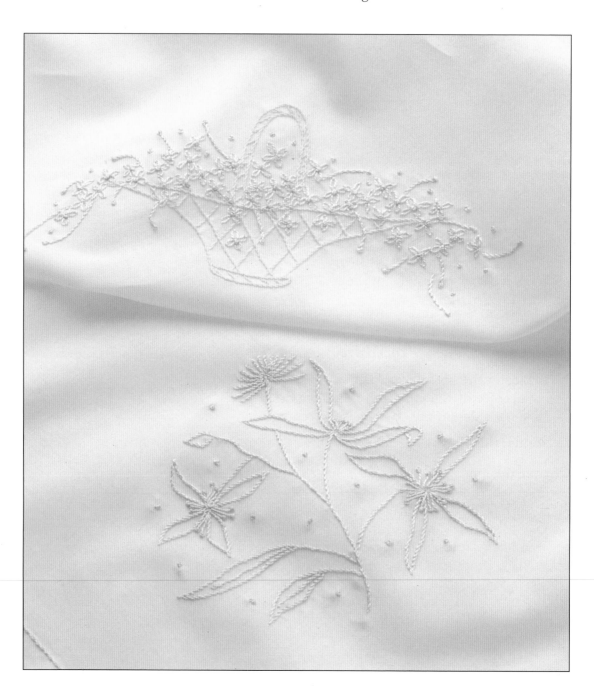

Rope Border Handtowel

CREAM ON CREAM

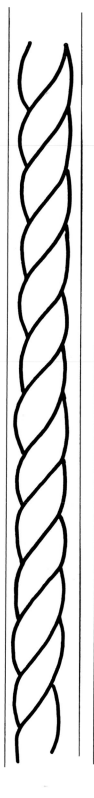

actual size

Materials

TOWEL

A purchased handtowel.

DECORATED STRIP

Homespun: 18" x 3 ¼ " (45 cm x 8 cm), or enough to fit your handtowel.

PIPING

Cream satin piping: 35 ½ " (90 cm), or enough to fit your handtowel.

Threads

Panda ™ Regal 4-ply Knitting and Crochet Cotton (55 cream)—or Cascade House Australia (cream).

Panda ™ Regal 2-ply Knitting and Crochet Cotton (ecru).

Procedure

1. Transfer the Rope Border design to the homespun (see Techniques), making sure the design is centred in the middle of the strip.

2. Stitch the design as follows:
    *   *outside rows, stem stitch (ecru)*
    *   *inside rows, coral stitch (ecru)*
    *   *rope row, colonial knots (cream).*

3. Cut the piping into two equal pieces. Pin a piece to each long side of the embroidered strip—right sides together. Sew in place.

4. Turn the edges to the wrong side, and press the seams under.

5. Pin the fabric strip to the towel, 2" (5 cm) from the bottom edge.

6. Tuck the ends of the strip in at the sides of the towel.

7. Sew the fabric strip in place by machine stitching in the ditch between the fabric and the piping on each side.

8. Hand sew the ends of the strip to the towel to close the gaps.

Strawberry Tea Towel

COLOUR ON CREAM

Materials

Cream waffle cloth: 27" x 25" (69 cm x 64 cm)—or a purchased, plain tea towel.

Strawberry print fabric: 25" x 3" (64 cm x 7.5 cm), or enough to fit across your tea towel.

Threads

DMC Perle no. 8 (644 ecru/grey).

EdMar Rayon Threads: Lola (050, 110 greens), (065, 211, reds) and (061 green and red).

Extras

Cream satin piping: 47" (120 cm), or enough to fit your tea towel.

Procedure

EMBROIDER THE DESIGN

1. Transfer the Strawberry Basket design onto the waffle cloth about 6" (15 cm) from the unhemmed bottom (see Techniques).

2. Stitch the design as follows:
    * *basket, stem stitch (644 ecru/grey)*
    * *handle, colonial knots (644 ecru/grey) double thread*
    * *leaves, continuous fly stitch (Lola 050, 110)*
    * *stems, back stitch (Lola 050, 110)*

Strawberries
    * *large middle strawberry, colonial knots (Lola 211 and 065 to highlight)*
    * *eight part-ripe and unripe small strawberries, colonial knots (Lola 061 green and red)*
    * *other strawberries, colonial knots (Lola 065) with edges in (Lola 211) for added dimension.*
    * *hull, detached chain stitch (Lola 050 and 110)*

HEM THE TEA TOWEL

3. Turn ¼" (0.5 cm) hems on the top and sides of the waffle cloth. Double the hems over again, and stitch them down.

4. Turn a ½" (1 cm) hem on the bottom of the waffle cloth. Double the hem over again, and stitch it down.

ATTACH THE PRINTED STRIP

5. Cut the piping into two equal pieces. Pin each piece (right sides together) to the long edges of the fabric strip. Sew in place.

6. Turn the edges to the back, and iron.

7. Pin the fabric strip to the towel 2" (5 cm) from the bottom edge.

8. Tuck the ends in at the sides of the towel.

9. Sew the fabric strip to the towel along the ditch between the fabric and the piping.

10. Hand sew the ends of the fabric strip to the tea towel.

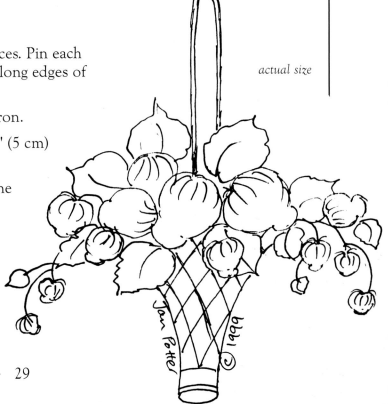

actual size

Wool Baby Blanket

CREAM ON CREAM

J Potter
© 1999

enlarge to 200% on a photocopier

Materials

Cream wool: 50" x 36" (125 cm x 90 cm).

Cream waffle fabric: 60" x 46" (155 cm x 120 cm)—or any backing fabric of your choice.

Threads

DMC Broder Medici Wool (white) and (ecru).

DMC Perle no. 8 (ecru).

Chenille Craftworks no. DJ188 (cream)—an acrylic knitting yarn.

Needle

For the chenille, use a large blunt needle such as is used for sewing knitted garments.

Backing fabric

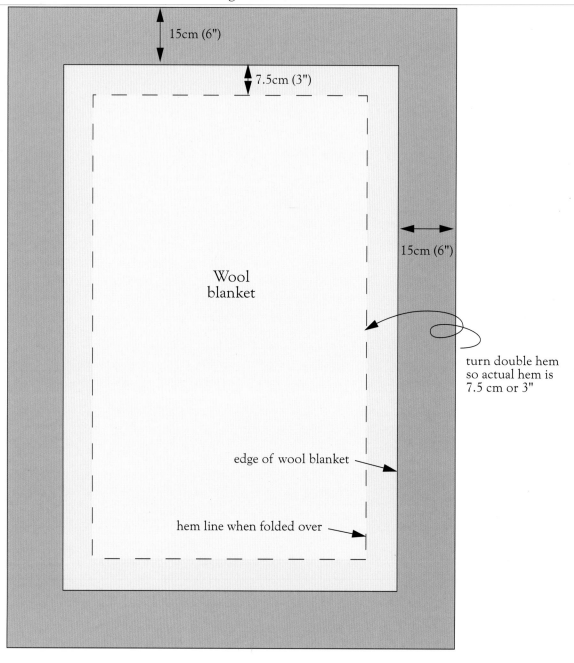

15cm (6")

7.5cm (3")

15cm (6")

Wool
blanket

turn double hem
so actual hem is
7.5 cm or 3"

edge of wool blanket

hem line when folded over

Extras

10" (25 cm) of 1 ½" (37 mm) wire edged cream silk
ribbon

Procedure

1. Transfer the Hearts for Baby design onto the cream
   wool fabric (see Techniques).

2. Stitch the design as follows:
   * *letters—outline, stem stitch (Medici Wool ecru) double
     thread*
     —fill, colonial knots (Chenille)
   * *large flowers—outline, stem stitch (Medici Wool white)
     double thread*
     —fill, long stitch (Chenille)
   * *small flowers, detached chain stitch (Medici Wool,
     white) double thread*
   * *flower centres, colonial knots (no. 8, ecru)*
   * *tendrils with dots at end, stem stitch with colonial knot
     (Medici Wool, ecru) double thread*
   * *heart, colonial knots (Chenille)*
   * *heart outline, stem stitch (Medici Wool ecru) double
     thread.*

3. Without making a knot, make three loops in the
   cream silk ribbon and stitch it to the centre top of
   the heart.

4. Iron the backing and the wool fabric.

5. Centre the blanket on the backing, wrong sides
   together.

6. Smooth both pieces flat, carefully making sure that
   both the vertical and horizontal grains of the
   backing fabric are straight.

7. Measure a 6" (15 cm) margin all around. Fold the
   four sides in to edge of blanket so they measure 3"
   (7.5 cm). Pin and press in the fold lines.

8. Fold the sides over so the hem measures 3" (7.5 cm).
   Pin and press.

9. Mitre the corners (see Techniques).

10. Hem by hand with blind hemming, catching only the
    blanketing.

Antique Flower Plate Cushion

COLOUR ON CREAM

Materials

Homespun 14" sq x 2 (36 cm sq x 2)

Threads

Panda ™ Regal 4-ply Knitting and Crochet Cotton: (55 cream), (828 pale green) and (R10 shaded brown, grey and cream—most of the cream was cut off to get a better brown effect).

Extras

10" (25 cm) zipper.

Procedure

1. Transfer the Antique Flower Plate design (page 21) onto the fabric (see Techniques).

2. Stitch the design as follows:
   - *flowers, continuous fly stitch (55 cream)*
   - *leaves, satin stitch (828 pale green)*
   - *stems, stem stitch (828 pale green)*
   - *border, close colonial knots (828 pale green and R10 sh. brown and grey), most of the dots, colonial knots (828 pale green)*
   - *centres of flowers, colonial knots (828 pale green)*
   - *random dots, colonial knots (R10, sh. brown and grey)*
   - *straight edges, stem stitch (R10, sh. brown and grey)*
   - *waves, stem stitch (828 pale green).*

4. Stitch the zipper into the bottom side of the cushion cover.

5. Sew up the remaining three sides of the cushion, right sides together.

6. You may wish to add frills, wadded decorations, tassels or cord around the edges.

Blue Fantasy Butterfly Cushion

CREAM ON CREAM

Materials

Homespun: 12½" sq x 2 (32 cm sq x 2).

Threads

Sullivans Candlewicking Thread (natural).

Panda ™ Regal 4-ply Knitting and Crocheting Cotton (55 cream), or Cascade House Australia (cream).

Extras

10" (25.5 cm) zipper

Procedure

1. Transfer the Blue Fantasy Butterfly design and the Large Gumleaf Frame design onto the centre of the fabric (see Techniques).

2. Stitch the designs as follows:

Butterfly design
   • *wings—full outline and lower wings, coral stitch (cream)*

enlarge to 200% on a photocopier

—large row of ovals at top, satin stitch (cream)
—ovals, 2nd row, colonial knots (cream)
—ribs of upper wing, stem stitch (cream)
• remaining upper wing dots, colonial knots (Sullivans natural)
• lower wing dots (cream)
• body, stem stitch (cream)
• body stripes, buttonhole stitch (cream)
• antennae, stem stitch with colonial knot at end (cream)

Frame
   • leaves, stem stitch (cream)
   • stems, colonial knots (cream).

3.   When the embroidery is finished, sew the zipper into the bottom seam of the cushion, and then sew up the sides.

4.   Turn the cushion cover right side out. You may wish to put frills, wadded decorations, tassels or cord around the edges.

actual size

Golden Sunshine Cushion

CREAM ON CREAM

J Potter © '99

enlarge to 200% on a photocopier

Materials

Homespun: 12½" sq (32 cm sq).

Threads

Sullivans Candlewicking Cotton (natural).

Extras

10" (25.5 cm) zipper.

Procedure

1. Transfer the Golden Sunshine Butterfly design onto the centre of the fabric and the Large Gumleaf Frame around the outside (see Techniques).

2. Stitch the design as follows:

actual size

Butterfly design
- *wings—top section, colonial knots*
- *—middle section, coral stitch*
- *—bottom section, stem stitch*
- *ovals in middle section, satin stitch*
- *body, stem stitch*
- *body stripes, buttonhole stitch*
- *eyes, colonial knots*
- *antennae, stem stitch with colonial knot at end*

Frame
- *leaves, stem stitch*
- *stems, colonial knots.*

3. When the embroidery is finished, sew the zipper into the bottom seam of the cushion, and then sew up the remaining seams.

4. Turn the cushion cover right side out. You may wish to put frills, wadded decorations, tassels or cord around the edges.

Bridal Veil Clematis Cushion

COLOUR ON CREAM

enlarge to 200% on a photocopier

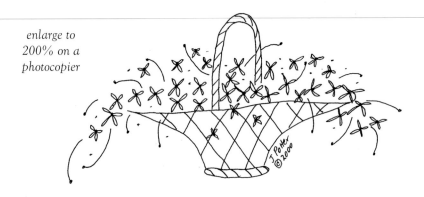

Materials

Homespun: 12" x 11" (30.5 cm x 28 cm).

Threads

EdMar Rayon Threads: Lola (048 pale green); Frost (028 variegated blue, pink peach, mauve) and (008 shaded yellow).

Extras

20" (50 cm) of ⅛" (3 mm) silk ribbon—optional

10" (25 cm) zipper

Procedure

1. Transfer the Bridal Veil Clematis Basket design onto the centre of the fabric and the Bridal Veil Clematis Corner design into the corners (see Techniques).

2. Stitch the design as follows:
   • *basket, stem stitch (Frost 008)*
   • *flowers—larger ones in corner design, satin stitch (Frost 028)*
   —smaller ones in corner and basket, detached chain stitch (Frost 028)
   —centres, colonial knots (Frost 008)
   • *tendrils—stem stitch, colonial knot at end (Frost 028)*
   • *leaves and dots, detached chain stitch and colonial knot (Lola 048).*
   • *buds, detached chain stitch (Frost 028).*

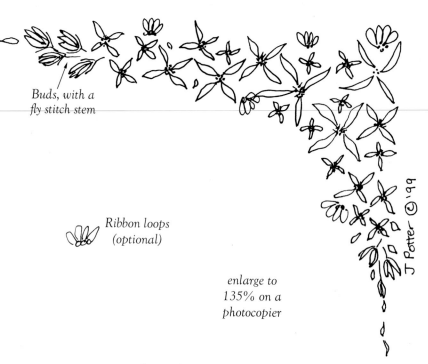

Buds, with a fly stitch stem

Ribbon loops (optional)

enlarge to 135% on a photocopier

J Potter © '99

• *stems, fly stitch (Lola 048).*
• *dots, colonial knots (Lola 048).*

3. If you wish, add looped ribbon decorations to the top left corner design.

4. When the embroidery is finished, sew the zipper into the bottom seam of the cushion, and then sew up the remaining seams.

5. Turn the cushion cover right side out. You may wish to put frills, wadded decorations, tassels or cord around the edges.

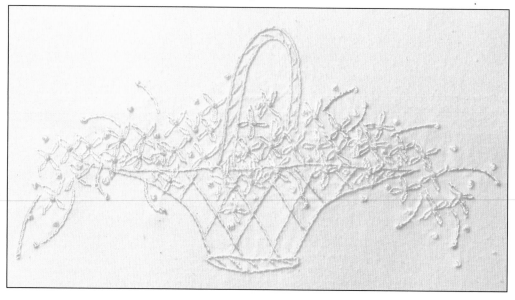

Bird House Cushion

COLOUR ON CREAM

Materials

Homespun: 11" x 13¾" (28 cm x 35 cm).

Drop shadow satin: 11" x 13¾" (28 cm x 35 cm).

Threads

DMC Perle no. 8 (92 variegated green).

Cascade House Australia Yarns (yellow).

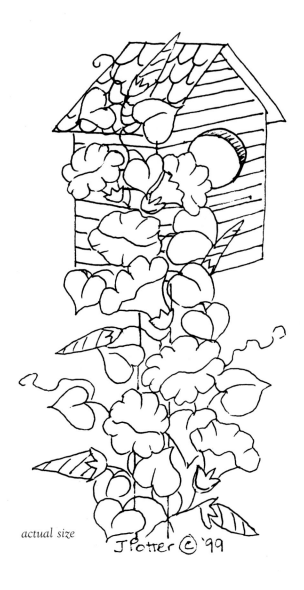

actual size

Sullivans Candlewicking Thread (natural).

Panda ™ Regal 4-ply Knitting and Crochet Cotton
(R14 variegated blue).

Extras

10" (25.5 cm) zipper

Procedure

1. Transfer the Bird House design and Leaf Border
   design onto the drop shadow satin (see Techniques).

2. Stitch the design as follows:

Central design
- *bird house and pole, stem stitch (yellow)*
- *flowers, buttonhole and stem stitch (R14 variegated
  blue)*
- *buds, buttonhole (R14 variegated blue)*
- *calyx, detached chain stitch (92 variegated green)*
- *leaves, stem stitch (92 variegated green)*
- *stems and tendrils, colonial knots (92 variegated green)*
- *hole, inside edge and edge, buttonhole and stem stitch
  continued around (natural)*
- *entry way, long stitch (natural)*
- *roof, stem stitch (natural)*

Border
- *leaves, stem stitch (R14 variegated green)*
- *stems, colonial knots (R14 variegated green).*

6. When the embroidery is finished, sew the zipper
   into the bottom seam of the cushion, and then
   sew up the remaining seams.

7. Turn the cushion cover right side out. You
   may wish to put frills, wadded
   decorations, tassels or cord around
   the edges.

actual size

Petunia Cushion

CREAM ON CREAM

Fabric

Linen: 21" sq x 2 (53 cm sq x 2).

Wadding: 14" sq (35 cm sq).

Calico backing: 14" (35 cm sq).

Threads

DMC Perle no. 8: (ecru) and (739 cream).

DMC Traditions (no. 5712 ecru).

Cascade House Australia (cream).

Panda™ Regal 4-ply Knitting and Crochet Cotton (R10 shaded grey/brown & cream).

Gütermann Quilting Cotton (cream).

enlarge to 200% on a photocopier

Extras

Annie Lane Designs cream ceramic cat button (sitting up)—or something similar.

A brass lion's head.

15½" or 16" (40 cm) zipper.

Procedure

1. Transfer the Petunia Garden Urn for Cushion design and the Rope Corner design onto the linen (see Techniques).

2. Stitch the designs as follows:

Central design
- *pedestal, inside front panel, colonial knots (Traditions ecru)*
- *bottom, sides and top, stem stitch (R10 shaded grey/brown & cream)*
- *gravel at base, colonial knots (R10 shaded grey/brown & cream)*
- *grass at base, colonial knots and long stitch (739 cream)*
- *urn, stem stitch (Cascade House cream)*
- *flowers, buttonhole and stem stitch (Traditions ecru, 739 cream)*
- *leaves and random dots, detached chain stitch and colonial knots (Perle no. 8 ecru)*

Border
- *outside rows, stem stitch (55 cream)*
- *inside rows, coral stitch (55 cream)*
- *rope row, stem stitch (55 cream)*

> **Tip:** It is easiest to do any colonial knots in a design last as the needle or thread tends to become caught in the raised knots. An embroidery hoop will flatten the knots if it is placed over them.

3. Only the embroidered area is quilted. See Techniques for how to assemble the quilt. Quilt around the inside and the outside of the border. Quilt around the outside of the pedestal and inside the front panel.

4. Sew the brass lion's head to the front of the pedestal, and sew the cat in the grass at the side of the pedestal.

5. Set the zipper into the bottom seam of the cushion, and then sew up the remaining seams.

6. Turn the cushion cover right side out. You may wish to put frills, wadded decorations, tassels or cord around the edges.

enlarge to 135% on a photocopier

Wedding Ring Cushions

CREAM AND COLOUR ON CREAM

This could also be cream on cream as there are only touches of colour.

Fabric

Drop shadow satin: tops and bottoms 8" x 6½" x 4 (20 cm x 16.5 cm x 4); and sides 29½" x 4" x 2 (75 cm x 10 cm x 2).

Drop shadow satin or bridal fabric: heart ring pocket 2"sq x 2 (5 cm sq x 2); and dangling hearts 2" x 2½" x 8 (5 cm x 6 cm x 8).

Wadding: 29½" x 14" x 2 (75 cm x 36 cm x 2).

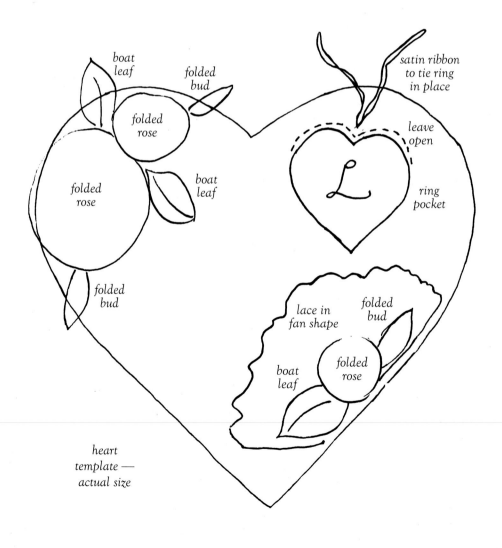

boat leaf

folded bud

folded rose

folded rose

boat leaf

folded bud

satin ribbon to tie ring in place

leave open

ring pocket

L

lace in fan shape

folded bud

boat leaf

folded rose

heart template — actual size

folded silk rose

dangling heart—actual size

ring pocket—actual size

Threads

EdMar Rayon Threads: Nova (159 cream); Frost (159 cream); and Iris (081 variegated dusty pink).

DMC stranded cotton (504 pale green) one strand only.

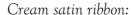

Extras

Silk ribbons:

- Blushing Bride, 96" x 1½" (2.40 m x 38 mm) for two 19½" (50 cm) large roses and four 13" (33 cm) medium roses.

- Blushing Bride, 20" x 1" (50 cm x 25 mm) for six folded rosebuds.

- Pine Needle, 24" x ½" (60 cm x 11 mm) for six boat leaves.

- Cherry Blossom, 24" x ½" (60 cm x 11 mm) for four small folded roses for dangling hearts.

Cream satin ribbon:

- bow for securing ring, 7¾" x ¼" x 2 (20 cm x 3 mm x 2)

- bow for dangling hearts, 10" x ¼" x 2 (25 cm x 3 mm x 2).

Cream satin twisted-cord piping 128" (3.20 m).

Muslin bag 12" x 5" x 2 (30 cm x 13 cm x 2).

Lavender: two sachets, or 1½ oz (42 g).

Procedure

1. Transfer the large heart shape onto the drop shadow satin tops; and the dangling hearts and ring pocket shapes onto the smaller pieces. Select initials from

enlarge to 200% on a photocopier

the cursive alphabet for the ring pocket and initials from the block alphabet for the dangling hearts (see Techniques).

2.   Stitch the design as follows:

Embroidery on tops
*   main heart, colonial knots (Nova 159 cream)*
*   ring pocket, buttonhole edge (Iris 081 dusty pink)*
*   initials on ring pockets, stem stitch (Iris 081 dusty pink)*
*   initials on dangling hearts, colonial knots (Frost 159 cream)*

3.   Fold the side strips of drop shadow satin in half to find the centre front, then transfer the front edge design so that it is centred on the line.

4.   Stitch the design as follows:

Central heart motif
*   heart, colonial knots (Nova 159 cream)*
*   flowers and buds, bullion stitch (Iris 081 dusty pink)*
*   calyx, fly stitch (504) one strand*
*   leaves, detached chain stitch (504) one strand*
*   dots, colonial knots (504) one strand*

Gumleaf sprays
*   stems, colonial knots (Frost 159 cream)*
*   leaves, stem stitch (Frost 159 cream)*
*   nuts, buttonhole and satin stitch (Iris 081 dusty pink)*

MAKING THE DECORATIONS

5.   After the embroidery is completed, make the folded roses, buds and boat leaves.

enlarge to 135%
on a photocopier

Folded rose

- *Roll the end of the ribbon five or six times to form the core of the rose.*
- *Stitch the roll at the base to hold the rose together.*
- *Fold the ribbon backwards on the diagonal. At the same time, roll the core further along the ribbon. Catch the base with a stitch. This forms one petal.*
- *Continue to fold and roll until the rose is the desired size. Keep pulling the core down so the petals are at the top. Catch with a stitch each time.*

Large rose = 15 or 16 folds

Medium rose = 8 or 9 folds

Small rose = 5 or 6 folds

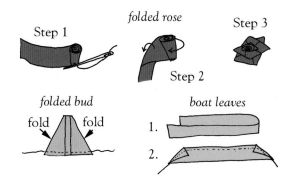

Folded bud

- *Fold the sides of the ribbon to the bottom edge.*
- *Sew running stitches across the edges just above the bottom.*
- *Gather a little and fold the sides together.*
- *Sew the bud in position under the rose.*

Boat leaves

- *Fold the ribbon in half, end to end.*
- *Fold the ends down a little more than halfway.*
- *Running stitch along the ribbon from one folded corner to the other folded corner. Pull up and gather a little, then end the stitching and turn to the right side.*
- *Attach the leaves under the rose at one end with two or three stitches.*

Dangling Hearts

- *Cut two hearts. Embroider initial on one heart. Sew them together by hand, leaving a gap to insert the stuffing. Turn to the right side.*

- *Stuff tightly by pushing small scraps of wadding in firmly. Sew up the gap.*
- *Sew a small rose in the dip of the heart.*
- *Sew one heart to one end of a 10″ x ¼″ (25 cm x 3 mm) cream satin ribbon.*
- *Sew the other heart to the other end of the ribbon.*
- *Make two loops in the ribbon and sew it to the top piece of the cushion.*

Make up each cushion

6. Follow the diagram for the placement of all the pieces. Stitch in place by hand in the following order: large rose; medium roses; folded buds; boat leaves; embroidered heart ring pocket; ribbon for securing the ring; and dangling hearts.

7. Pin the twisted-satin cord piping around the top and bottom sections, making sure the joins are at the back of the heart.

8. Machine the piping in place.

9. Snip to spread the seam allowance at the corners.

10. Pin the gusset to the top, right sides together, sandwiching the piping between the pieces. Keep the dangling hearts clear of the seam.

11. Sew around the edge.

12. Attach the bottom of the cushion similarly leaving a gap to insert the wadding and lavender.

13. Turn the cushion cover to the right side. Fill the cushion with wadding and lavender.

14. Sew the gap closed by hand.

Sampler Needle Book

CREAM ON CREAM

Finished size when closed: 5¼" x 4½" (13.5 cm x 11.5 cm)

Materials

Hemp: cover 9½" x 6 ⅛" (24 cm x 15.5 cm);
inside lining 9½" x 6 ⅛" (24 cm x 15.5 cm); and
pockets 9½" x 3¼" (24 cm x 8 cm).

Wool: 8½" x 5" (22 cm x 13 cm).

Wadding: 9½" x 6 ⅛" (24 cm x 15.5 cm).

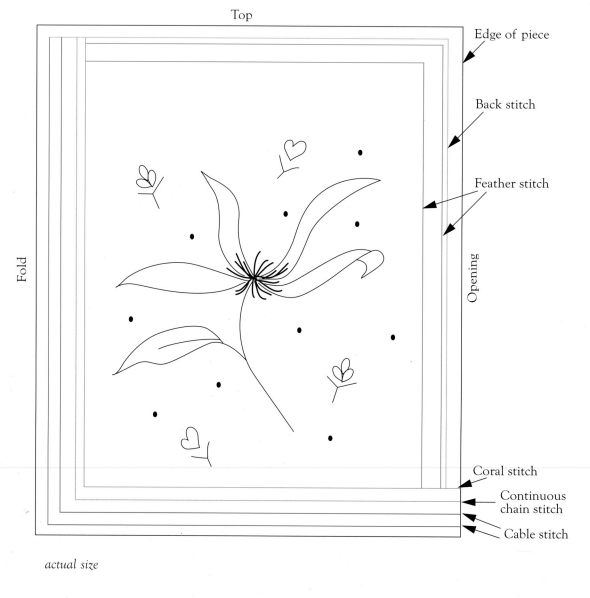

Top

Edge of piece

Back stitch

Feather stitch

Opening

Fold

Coral stitch

Continuous chain stitch

Cable stitch

actual size

Threads

FOR EMBROIDERY

DMC Traditions 100% Mercerised Crochet Cotton
(5712 ecru).

DMC Perle no. 8 (ecru).

FOR TWISTED CORD

5½ yd (5 m) DMC Traditions (ecru)—the cord will be
approximately 20" (50 cm).

Procedure

1. Fold the hemp cover fabric in half to mark the
    centre of the book. Transfer the Sampler Needle
    Book design onto the front (see Techniques). You
    may also wish to sign your name, initials and or date
    in the bottom panel.

2. Embroider the design as follows:

clematis design
   - *petals, whipped stem stitch (5712 ecru)*
   - *leaf, continuous fly stitch (5712 ecru)*
   - *stem, stem stitch (5712 ecru)*
   - *stamens, pistil stitch (5712 ecru)*
   - *dots, colonial knots (5712 ecru)*
   - *hearts, satin stitch (5712 ecru)*
   - *buds, detached chain (5712 ecru)*
   - *calyx, fly stitch (5712 ecru)*

Frame lines
   - *blue, cable stitch (5712 ecru)*
   - *grey, continuous chain stitch (5712 ecru)*
   - *red, coral stitch (5712 ecru)*
   - *brown, back stitch (5712 ecru)*
   - *green, feather stitch (5712 ecru)*

Signature
   - *signature, initials and or date, stem stitch (Perle
     no. 8 ecru).*

3. Blanket stitch the edges of the piece of wool.

4. Fold the wool in half—like a book—and iron
    the centre fold.

5. On the top long side of the pocket fabric,
    machine a small hem.

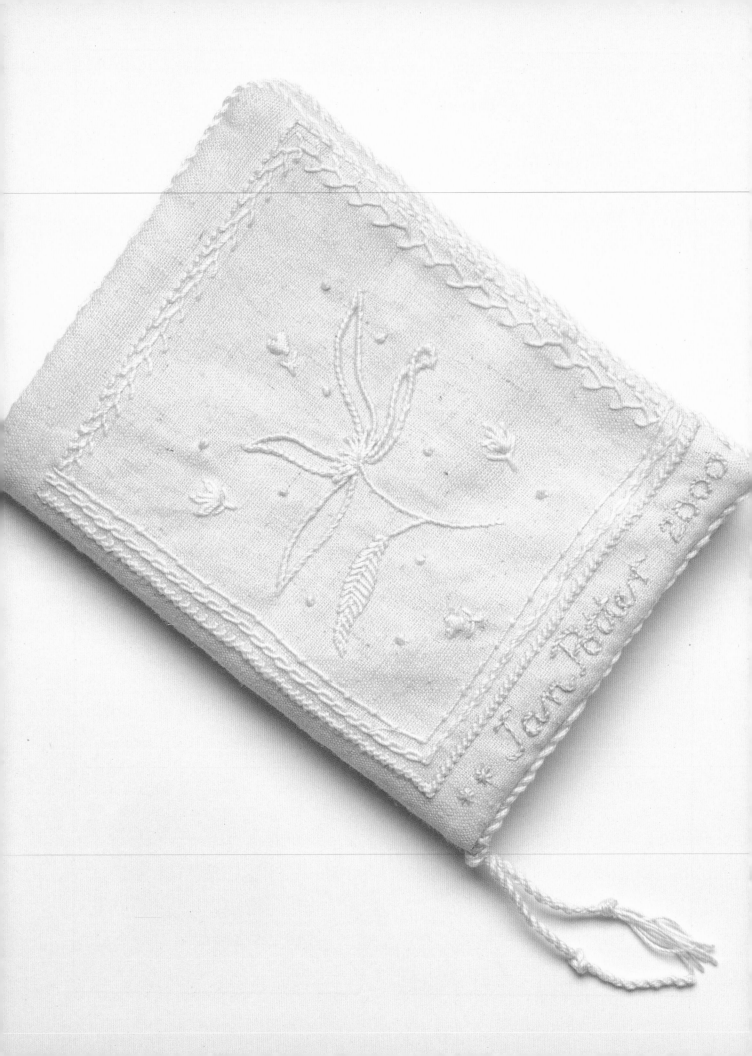

6. Sew the pocket to the lower half of the lining fabric.

7. Fold the lining in half—like a book—and iron the centre fold.

8. Lay the wool piece inside the lining, matching up the centre folds, and machine sew, in straight stitch, down the centre fold.

9. Layer the pieces, from the bottom, in the following order:
   • *wadding*
   • *lining with pockets and wool, right side up*
   • *embroidered piece, right side down. (Embroidery should be facing the wool on the left side.)*

10. Pin the layers together along the sides and the top, making sure that the edges of the embroidery are parallel to the pin line.

11. CHECK that the embroidery is placed correctly by turning the piece to the right side. If all is fine, proceed. Otherwise, correct the mistake.

12. Overlock (or zigzag and straight stitch) the pieces together, leaving a 2" (5 cm) gap in the centre of the bottom seam.

13. Pull the work to the right side, making sure all the corners are pushed out sharply.

14. Sew up the gap by hand.

15. Iron the needle book between two layers of towel, making sure the edges are flat.

16. Make a twisted cord (see Techniques). Knot the ends of the twisted cord. Hand sew the cord around the book, starting from the top centre and finishing at the bottom centre. You should have enough left to make a knot with dangling tails.

Shades of Lace Tea-cosy

COLOUR ON CREAM

Materials

Homespun (or tea-dyed lawn): 25½" x 20" (65 cm x 50 cm).

Wadding: 25½" x 10" (65 cm x 25 cm).

Threads

FOR EMBROIDERY

Panda ™ Regal 4-ply Knitting and Crochet Cotton (R13 shaded pink, mauves, blues and green).

FOR CORD

Panda™ Regal 4-ply Knitting and Crochet Cotton (R13)—two lengths of 164" (4.2 m) to make two 16½" (42 cm) cords.

Procedure

EMBROIDER THE DESIGN

1. Fold the homespun in half, lengthways; then fold the ends towards the middle.

2. Place the tea-cosy pattern on the fabric with the centre on the fold. Cut through four layers of fabric to make two ovals.

1a   Homespun

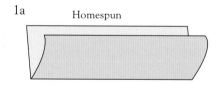

1b

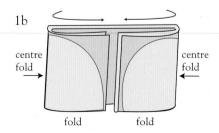

centre fold   centre fold

fold   fold

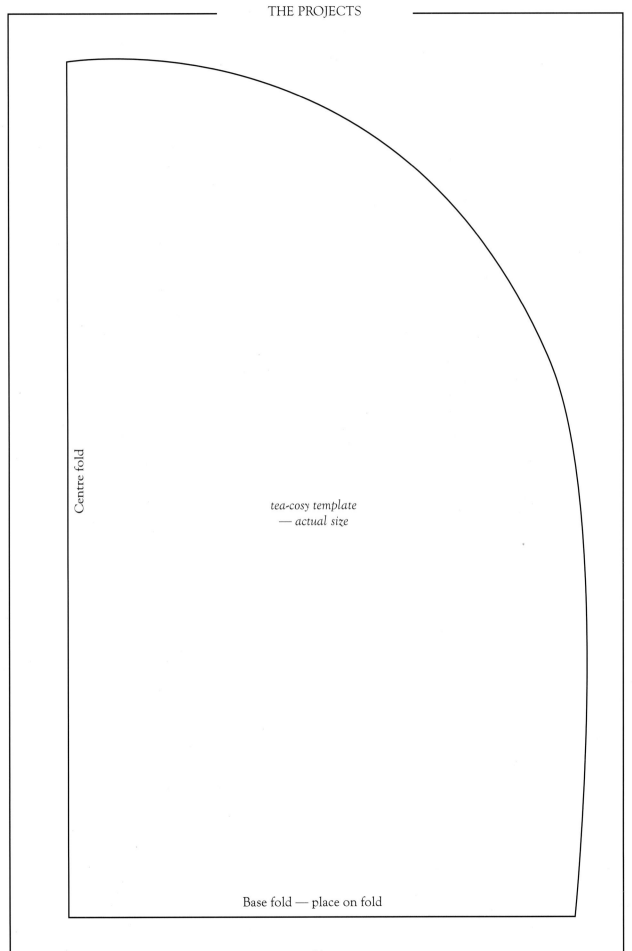

Centre fold

tea-cosy template
— actual size

Base fold — place on fold

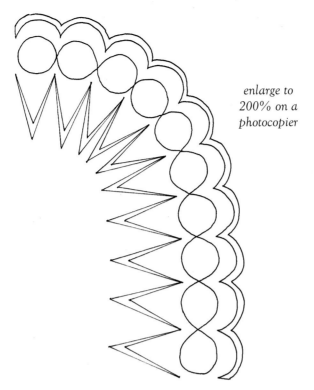

enlarge to 200% on a photocopier

3. Fold one of the ovals in half lengthwise. Match the Tea-cosy Lace Border design up to the centre line, and transfer it onto the fabric. Flip the design over, match it up to the centre line again and transfer it onto the other side of the arch.

Note: The design should fit into the arch leaving a seam allowance of about ½" (1 cm) to the edge of the fabric.

4. Stitch the design as follows:
   • *arrows, stem stitch*
   • *circles, spaced colonial knots*
   •*scallops, coral stitch.*

Assemble the tea-cosy

5. Fold the sides of the wadding piece to the centre. Lay the pattern with the centre on the fold, and cut along the curved line to produce two semicircles of wadding.

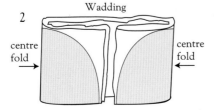

Wadding

2

centre fold

centre fold

6. Make a wadding sandwich by folding the homespun in half along the base (embroidery on the outside) and placing a semicircle of wadding inside. Stitch along the base of the wadding (so that it doesn't bunch up in the wash).

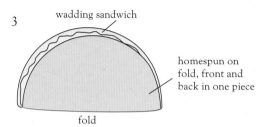

3 wadding sandwich

homespun on fold, front and back in one piece

fold

7. Overlock (or straight stitch and zigzag) the three layers together along the curved edge.

8. Make the other wadding sandwich the same way.

9. With the right sides together, sew the sandwiches together leaving holes for a teapot handle and a spout.

10. While the tea-cosy is inside out, sew the seams in the openings to the lining.

11. Turn the tea-cosy right side out.

Add a twisted cord

12. Follow the instructions in Techniques to make two cords.

13. Stitch the ends of the cords to the seam inside the tea-cosy.

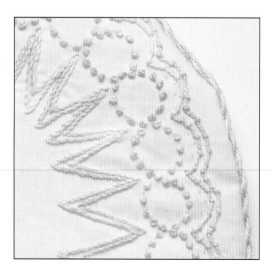

14. Hand sew the cords along the outside seam. When you get to the centre top, there should be enough cord to make a bow. I have left the bow without tails so that they won't clutter the embroidery.

Violet Border Tea-cosy

COLOUR ON CREAM

Materials

FOR TEA-COSY

Homespun: 25½" x 20" (65 cm x 50 cm).

Wadding: 25½" x 10" (65 cm x 25 cm).

FOR TOP DECORATION

Homespun: 27½" x 5½" (70 cm x 14 cm).

Wadding: 27½" x 4" (70 cm x 10 cm).

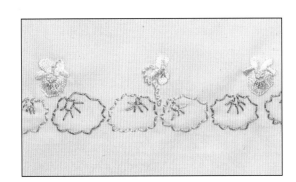

Threads

FOR EMBROIDERY

EdMar Rayon Threads: Glory (081 pale mauve); Lola (050 shaded green); Frost (080 shaded green) and (069 shaded pale yellow)

Rajmahal Silk (dark pink).

FOR CORD

EdMar Rayon Thread: Iris (081 shaded pale mauve)—one 16yd (15 m) skein to make one 20" (50 cm) cord.

Procedure

EMBROIDER THE DESIGN

1. Fold the homespun in half, lengthways; then fold the ends towards the middle.

2. Place the tea-cosy pattern upright on the folded fabric with the centre on the fold. Cut along the curved line to produce two ovals.

3. Fold the fabric in half along the baseline and transfer the Violet Border design onto the fabric. Make sure there is at least ½" (1 cm) between the edge of the design and the baseline.

4. Stitch the design as follows:
   • *violet top petals, satin stitch (Glory 081)*
   • *violet lower petals, buttonhole stitch (Glory 081)*

1a Homespun

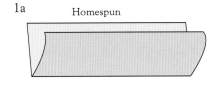

1b

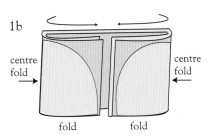

- *leaves, back stitch (Lola 050)*
- *stems, close colonial knots (Frost 080)*
- *stamen, colonial knots (Frost 069)*
- *lines on violet, long stitch (Two strands of Rajmahal Silk).*

ASSEMBLE THE WADDING SANDWICHES

5. Fold the sides of the wadding piece to the centre. Lay the pattern on the wadding with the centre on the fold, and cut to produce two semicircles of wadding.

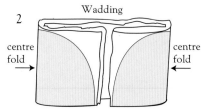

6. Make a wadding sandwich by folding the homespun in half along the base (embroidery on the outside) and placing a semicircle of wadding inside. Stitch along the base of the wadding (so that it doesn't bunch up in the wash).

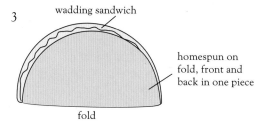

7. Overlock (or straight stitch and zigzag) the three layers together along the curved edge.

8. Make the other wadding sandwich the same way.

TO MAKE THE TWISTED CORD

9. First undo the knot and open the skein of thread right out to form one huge loop. Follow instructions for making twisted cord (see Techniques).

actual size

TO MAKE THE WADDING DECORATION

10. Roll the wadding inside the length of homespun fabric. Squeeze the wadding into the tube about 1" (2.5 cm) in diameter, leaving about a 1" strip of homespun to sew. Pin the fabric tightly together along the edge of the wadding. Overlock (or straight stitch and zigzag) below the pins—trim off the excess.

11. Turn in the ends of the wadded decoration, and sew them closed by hand.

12. Use an awl to punch six evenly spaced holes along the seam base of the wadded decoration between the seam and the wadding. Make the first and last holes 3" (8 cm) in from the ends.

13. Hand stitch one end of the twisted cord to one end of the roll between the pins and the edge.

14. Pull the cord through the holes using a crochet hook, wrapping it around the wadded decoration as you go. Hand stitch the other end of the cord to the other end of the wadded decoration.

15. Adjust the loops to sit evenly.

TO ASSEMBLE THE TEA-COSY

16. Pin the edge of the wadded decoration to the edge of the right side of the embroidered sandwich, and machine it in place.

17. Pin the other sandwich on top (leaving the wadded decoration in the middle).

18. Leaving holes for a teapot spout and handle, machine the pieces together, covering the previous seam lines but without stitching into the wadding or twisted cord.

19. Hand sew the seams in the openings to the inside lining.

20. Turn the tea-cosy right side out.

Blue Fantasy Butterfly Miniature Quilt

COLOUR ON CREAM

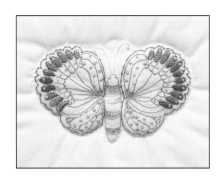

Materials

Homespun: 11" x 10" (28 cm x 25.5 cm).

Calico backing: 11" x 10" (28 cm x 25.5 cm.

Wadding: 11" x 10" (28 cm x 25.5 cm).

Drop shadow satin binding: 12" x 1½" x 2 (31 cm x 4 cm x 2); and 10½" x 1½" x 2 (27 cm x 4 cm x 2).

Threads

EdMar Rayon Thread: Iris (145 peacock blue), (219 light blue) and (220 denim blue).

Extras

Small blue applique butterfly. (I found this one in an antique shop.)

Procedure

1. Transfer the Blue Fantasy Butterfly design and the Large Gumleaf Frame onto the homespun (see Techniques).

2. Stitch the designs as follows:

Butterfly
   • *wings—full outline, coral stitch (145 peacock blue)*
   —large row of ovals at top, satin stitch (145 peacock blue)
   —second row of ovals, stem stitch (220 denim blue)
   —upper and lower wing ribs, coral stitch (220 denim blue)
   —dots, colonial knots (219 light blue)

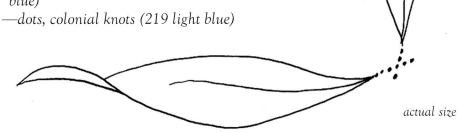

actual size

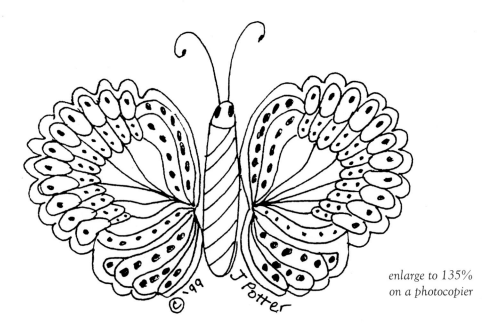

enlarge to 135%
on a photocopier

       • *body, stem stitch around (219 light blue)*
       • *bars on body, buttonhole stitch (219 light blue)*
       • *antennae, stem stitch with colonial knot on end (219*
         light blue)

Frame
       • *leaves, stem stitch (219 light blue)*
       • *stems, candlewicking knots (219 light blue).*

3.   Follow the quilting directions in Techniques to assemble the backing, wadding and fabric.

4.   Quilt around the large gumleaves and stems.

5.   Quilt about ¼" (0.5 cm) out from—and all around—the butterfly.

6.   When the quilting is complete, bind the quilt by following the directions in Techniques.

7.   After the binding is completed, attach the small blue appliqué butterfly to the top right leaf in the border.

Golden Sunshine Miniature Quilt

COLOUR ON CREAM

actual size

Materials

Homespun: 11" x 10" (28 cm x 25.5 cm).

Calico backing: 11" x 10" (28 cm x 25.5 cm).

Wadding: 11" x 10" (28 cm x 25.5 cm).

Drop Shadow Satin binding: 12" x 1½" x 2 (31 cm x 4 cm x 2); and 10½" x 1½" x 2 (27 cm x 4 cm x 2).

Threads

EdMar Rayon Threads: Lola (203 orange gold), (059 shaded brown); Frost (069 shaded pale yellow), (008 shaded yellow) and (080 shaded green).

Extras

Four brass butterflies.

Procedure

1. Transfer the Golden Sunshine Butterfly design and the Gumleaf Frame design onto the homespun (see Techniques).

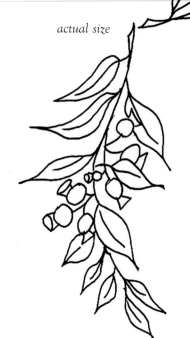

actual size

2. Stitch the designs as follows:

Butterfly

- *wings—top and middle sections, stem stitch (Frost 069)*
  —bottom section, stem stitch (Frost 008)
  —top wing section, colonial knots along ribs (Lola 203)
  —middle wing section, satin stitch in ovals (Lola 203)
- *body—stem stitch around body (Lola 059)*
- *bars on body, buttonhole stitch (Lola 059)*
- *eyes, colonial knots (Lola 059)*
- *antennae, stem stitch with colonial knot at end (Lola 059)*

Frame

- *leaves, stem stitch (Frost 080)*
- *stems, colonial knots (Frost 080)*
- *nuts, round part in satin stitch, flared part in buttonhole stitch (Lola 059).*

3. See Techniques for how to begin quilting.

4. Quilt along the main stem only of the border. Quilt about ¼" (0.5 cm) out from—and all around—the butterfly.

5. Bind the quilt following the directions in Techniques.

6. After completing the quilt, sew the brass butterflies in the corners, where the stems of the gumleaf sprays join.

Bird House Miniature Quilt

CREAM ON CREAM

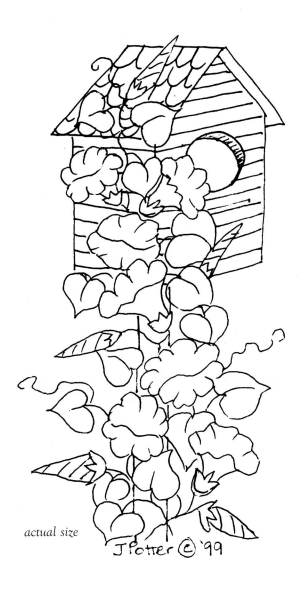

actual size

J Potter © '99

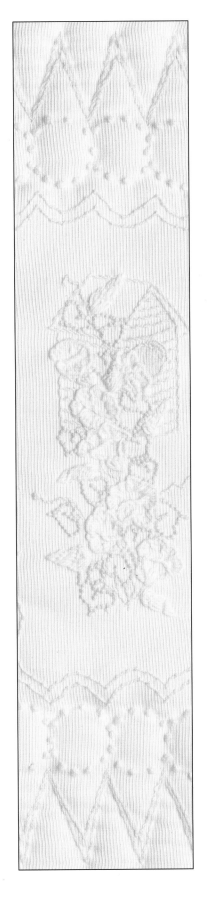

Materials

Drop shadow satin: 11" x 13 ½" (28 cm x 35 cm.)

Calico backing: 11" x 13½" (28 cm x 35 cm).

Wadding: 11" x 13½" (28 cm x 35 cm).

Drop shadow satin binding: 15½" x 1½" x 2 (40 cm x 4 cm x 2); and 12½" x 1½" x 2 (32 cm x 4 cm x 2).

Threads

Cascade House Australia (cream).

DMC Perle no. 8 (ecru).

Extras

Four small brass bird houses.

Procedure

1. Transfer the Bird House and Morning Glories design and the Lace Border design onto the drop shadow satin (see Techniques).

2. Stitch the designs as follows:

Central design
-   *bird house and post, stem stitch (ecru)*
-   *leaves, colonial knots (ecru)*
-   *buds, buttonhole stitch (cream)*

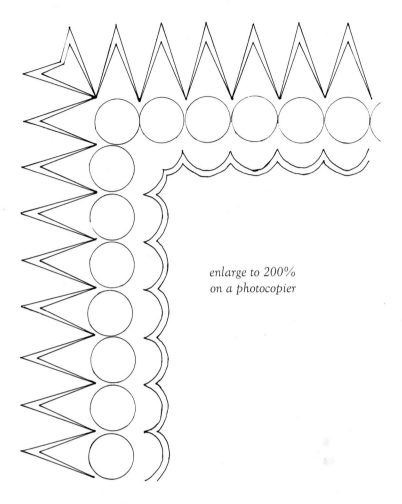

*enlarge to 200%
on a photocopier*

- *calyx, detached chain stitch (cream)*
- *flowers, buttonhole stitch and stem stitch (cream)*
- *stems, stem stitch (cream)*
- *tendrils, stem stitch (ecru)*

Border
- *arrows, stem stitch (ecru)*
- *circles, spaced colonial knots (cream)*
- *scallops, coral stitch (ecru).*

3. Follow the quilting instructions in Techniques.

4. Quilt around the outside edge of the arrow border and the outer edge of the bottoms of the circles facing the bird house.

5. Bind the quilt using the instructions in Techniques.

6. Sew one brass bird house in each corner of the finished quilt.

Petunia Miniature Quilt

COLOUR ON CREAM

*enlarge to 200%
on a photocopier*

Materials

Drop shadow satin: 13 ½" x 11" (35 cm x 28 cm).

Calico backing: 13½" x 11" (35 cm x 28 cm).

Wadding: 13½" x 11" (35 cm x 28 cm).

Drop shadow satin binding: 12¾" x 1½" x 2 (32.5 cm x 4 cm x 2); and 11" x 1½" x 2 (28 cm x 4 cm x 2).

Threads

DMC Traditions (ecru).

DMC Perle no. 8 (92 variegated green).

Panda ™ Regal 4-ply Knitting and Crochet Cotton (R10 variegated brown).

EdMar Rayon Threads: Lola (070, 041, 127 mauve shades); and Frost (080 variegated green).

Extras

Brass lion's head—or something similar.

Annie Lane Designs terracotta lying-down-cat button—or something similar.

Procedure

1. Transfer the Petunia Garden Urn design onto the drop shadow satin (see Techniques).

2. Draw three rectangular borders around the outside, to the following measurements:
    - *inner 10 ¼" x 6" (26 cm x 15 cm)*
    - *middle 9 ¼" x 6 ¾" (23.5 cm x 17 cm)*
    - *outer 8" x 7 ⅝" (20.5 cm x 19.5 cm).*

3. Stitch the design as follows:

Central design
- *pedestal—front panel, colonial knots (Traditions ecru)*
  —bottom, sides and top, stem stitch (R10 variegated brown)
- *gravel at base, colonial knots (R10 variegated brown)*
- *grass at base, colonial knot and long stitch (92 variegated green)*
- *flowers, buttonhole and stem stitch (Lola mauve shades)*
- *leaves and random dots, detached chain stitch and candlewicking stitch (Frost 080 variegated green)*

Border
- *inner, coral stitch (92 variegated green)*
- *middle, coral stitch (041 lilac)*
- *outer, coral stitch (ecru)*

4. After embroidery is completed, sew the brass lion's head to the front of the pedestal, and sew the cat in grass at the side of the pedestal.

5. See Techniques for how to assemble the quilt backing, wadding and embroidered top.

6. Quilt around the outside edge of the frame, close to the stitches.

7. Bind and hang the quilt (see Techniques).

Strawberry Basket Miniature Quilt

CREAM ON CREAM

actual size

Materials

Homespun: 11" sq (28 cm sq).

Calico backing: 11" sq (28 cm sq).

Wadding: 11" sq (28 cm sq).

Drop shadow satin binding: 12" x 1½" x 4
(31 cm x 4 cm x 4).

Threads

DMC Perle no. 8 (deep ecru).

EdMar Rayon Threads Nova (159 cream).

Cascade House Australia Traditional Candlewicking Cotton (cream).

DMC stranded cotton (543 cream).

Extras

Four large wooden heart beads.

Two 6" x ¾" (15 cm x 2 cm) scraps of drop shadow satin for corner ties.

Procedure

1. Transfer the Strawberry Basket design and the Leaf Border design onto the homespun (see Techniques).

2. Stitch the design as follows:
    * *basket, candlewicking knots (deep ecru)*
    * *leaves, continuous fly stitch (543 cream) three strands*
    * *stems, back stitch (543 cream) three strands*

Strawberries
    * *large middle strawberry (Cascade House cream) two strands*
    * *largish berry on each side (Nova 159 cream)*
    * *all other berries (Cascade House cream) one strand*
    * *hull, detached chain stitch (543 cream) three strands*

Frame
    * *leaves, stem stitch (deep ecru)*
    * *stems, colonial knot (deep ecru)*

Embroider in this order: basket; leaves; all smaller berries; largish berries; and large middle berry.

3. See Techniques for how to begin the quilting.

4. Use colonial knots to quilt, making diamonds at the centre of each edge and triangles at the corners of the leaf border.

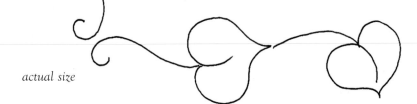

actual size

5. Bind the quilt (see Techniques).

6. Place Cascade House Australia cream thread ties 2"
   (5 cm) diagonally in from the corner border.

7. Sew the wooden heart beads in the corners, with the
   points facing to the centre of the quilt.

8. Knot the drop shadow satin scraps in the centre, clip
   the tails and sew them above the hearts on the top
   corners.

Surprise Christmas Miniature Quilt

CREAM ON CREAM

Materials

Homespun: 10" sq (25.5 cm sq).

Calico backing: 10" sq (25.5 cm sq).

Wadding: 10" sq (25.5 cm sq).

Floral cotton patchwork fabric: 10¼" x 1½" x 4 (26 cm x 4 cm x 4)—for binding.

Threads

DMC Perle no. 8 (ecru).

Cascade House Australia (cream).

Extras

Nine pearl beads.

Seven antique bugle beads

Six gold beads (Mill Hill 20557).

½" (1 cm) diameter brass star.

Ribbons:
- *cream silk, ⅛" x 8" (3 mm x 20 cm) plus (3 mm x 10 cm)—for candy stick*
- *Blushing Bride hand dyed silk, ⅜" x 4" (10 cm x 11 mm)—for candle*
- *cream silk, ⅛" x 8" (3 mm x 20 cm)—for gift box*

Procedure

EMBROIDER THE DESIGN

1. Transfer the Surprise Christmas Mini Quilt design onto the homespun (see Techniques).

Stitch the design as follows:
- *all border lines, stem stitch (Cascade House cream)*
- *snow flakes or random dots (in border), colonial knots (Cascade House cream)*

actual size

J Potter © 2000

- *snowflakes in squares, stem stitch and colonial knot at end (ecru)*
- *candle—outline, stem stitch (ecru)*
—stripes, silk ribbon held down by colonial knots (ecru)
- *leaves, continuous fly stitch (ecru)*
- *flower, colonial knots (ecru)*
- *candy stick—stripes, two rows of chain stitch (ecru)*
—outline, stem stitch (ecru)
—silk ribbon held down by colonial knot (ecru)
- *Christmas tree—three triangles, continuous fly stitch (ecru)*
—trunk, three satin stitches (ecru)
- *holly leaves, continuous fly stitch (ecru)*
- *gift box—outline, stem stitch (ecru)*
—wrapping ribbon, three rows of chain stitch (ecru)

Make the ribbons

3. To make the ribbon bow on the candy stick: make five loops with two tails ⅝" (15 mm) long each. From the ⅛" x 4" (3 mm x 10 cm) piece, make one loop of ⁵⁄₁₆" (14 mm) with two tails. Sew the two bows together—through the bit where the loops meet—to the candy stick, using ecru thread and colonial knots.

4. To make the ribbon flower on the candle: fold the silk ribbon in half, lengthwise. Sew running stitches along the pink edge. Gather up the ribbon to the desired size and attach it in place over the flower on the design. Sew a pearl bead into the centre.

5. To make the ribbon bow on the gift box: make five loops and two tails. Attach the bow to the gift box with colonial knots in ecru thread

Attach the extras

6. Make each candle for tree by sewing on a gold bead and an antique bugle bead together.

7. Make the flame on the candle with a bugle bead.

8. Sew on the remaining eight pearl beads for holly berries.

9. Attach the brass star to the top of the Christmas tree.

Finishing the mini quilt

10. See Techniques for how to begin the quilting.

11. Quilt along the outside edges of the snowflake border and the outside edge of the main square containing the boxes.

12. Quilt small circles or triangles where the box corners meet.

13. Bind and hang the mini quilt (see Techniques).

Peace Banner

COLOUR ON CREAM

*enlarge to 200%
on a photocopier*

Materials

Homespun: 13" x 6" (33 cm x 15 cm).

Calico backing: 13" x 6" (33 cm x 15 cm).

Wadding: 13" x 6" (33 cm x 15 cm).

Outer backing fabric of your choice: 11½" x 5" (30 cm x 13 cm)—optional.

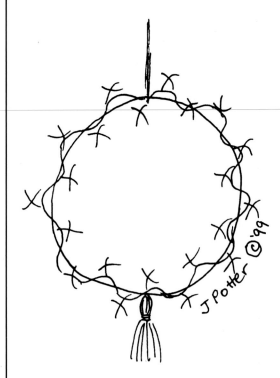

Threads

DMC Metallic Thread Perle no. 5 (5282 gold).

DMC stranded cotton (818 pink).

Panda™ Regal 4-ply Knitting and Crochet Cotton (64 pale pink) and (215 ecru).

Cascade House Australia Traditional Candlewicking Cotton (cream).

Extras

Dark gold twisted cord piping 32" (80 cm).

35 gold beads (Mill Hill 20557)—for flower centres.

Dark gold tassel: 3½" (9 cm)—to hang from centre point.

Procedure

1. Transfer the Bridal Veil Circlet Banner design onto the homespun (see Techniques).

2. Stitch the designs as follows:
   • *circle, colonial knots (cream)*
   • *leaf circlet, featherstitch (818 pink)*
   • *clematis flowers, detached chain stitch (5282 gold)*
   • *random dots, colonial knots (5282 gold)*
   • *letters, whipped stem stitch—base colour (64 pale pink), whip colour (5282 gold)*
   • *borders, stem stitch—inside (215 ecru)*
   —outside (cream).

3. See Techniques for how to begin the quilting.

4. Quilt the outside and inner edge of the border.

5. Quilt around the circle of colonial knots.

6. See Techniques for how to finish and hang the banner. The outer backing is optional.

Joy Banner

COLOUR ON CREAM

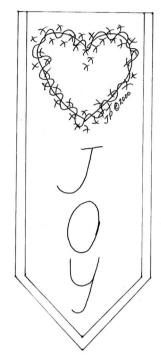

*enlarge to 200%
on a photocopier*

Materials

Homespun: 9" x 5½" (23 cm x 14 cm).

Calico backing: 9" x 5 ½" (23 cm x 14 cm).

Wadding: 9" x 5 ½" (23 cm x 14 cm).

Outer backing fabric of your choice: 8½" x 4½" (21 cm x 11 cm)—optional.

Threads

DMC Metallic Thread Perle no. 5 (5282 gold).

DMC stranded cotton (503 pale green).

Panda™ Regal 4-ply Knitting and Crochet Cotton (828 pale green and 215 ecru).

Cascade House Australia (cream).

Extras

33 gold beads (Mill Hill 20557)—for flower centres.

Dark gold twisted cord piping 25½" (65 cm)

Dark gold tassel 3½" (9 cm)—to hang from the centre point

Procedure

1. Transfer the Bridal Veil Clematis Heart Banner design onto the homespun (see Techniques).

2. Stitch the design as follows:
    • *heart, candlewicking knots (Cascade House cream)*
    • *leaf circlet, featherstitch (503 pale green)*
    • *clematis flowers, detached chain stitch (5282 Gold)*
    • *random dots, colonial knots (5282 Gold)*
    • *letters, whipped stem stitch—base colour (828 pale green), whip colour (5282 gold)*
    • *borders, stem stitch (215 ecru)*

3. See Techniques for how to start quilting.

4. Quilt the outside and inner edge of the border.

5. Quilt around the circle of colonial knots.

6. See Techniques for how to finish and hang the banner.

Noel Banner

COLOUR ON CREAM

Materials

Homespun: 20" x 6" (51 cm x 15 cm).

Calico backing: 20" x 6" (51 cm x 15 cm).

Wadding: 20" x 6" (51 cm x 15 cm).

Outer backing fabric of your choice: 16" x 5½" (41 cm x 14 cm)—optional.

Threads

Panda ™ Regal 4-ply Knit and Crochet Cotton: (R10 variegated brown); and (828 grey green).

Cascade House Australia (cream).

DMC Metallic Perle no. 5 (5282 dark gold).

DMC Perle no. 5 (light pink, dark green).

Extras

Nine pearl beads.

Seven antique bugle beads.

13 gold beads (Mill Hill 20557).

½" (1 cm) diameter brass star.

Brass Christmas tree.

Cream twisted cord piping 45" (115 cm).

Ribbons:

> • cream silk, ⅛" x 8" (3 mm x 20 cm) plus ⅛" x 4" (3 mm x 10 cm)—for candy stick
> • Blushing Bride hand dyed silk, ⅜" x 4" (11 cm x 10 mm)—for candle
> • pink organza ribbon, ⁵⁄₁₆" x 6" (7 mm x 15 cm)—for gift box

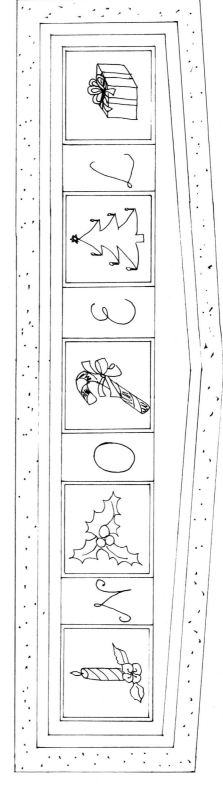

enlarge to 200% on a photocopier

Procedure

EMBROIDER THE DESIGN

1. Transfer the Surprise Christmas Mini Quilt design onto the homespun (see Techniques).

2. Stitch the design as follows:
    - *box outlines, stem stitch (Cascade House cream)*
    - *all borders, stem stitch (R10 variegated brown)*
    - *snowflake border, colonial knots (Cascade House cream)*
    - *letters, stem stitch (5282 dark gold)*
    - *candle—outline, stem stitch (Cascade House cream)*
    - *—stripes, chain stitch (Perle no. 5 light pink)*
    - *—leaves, continuous fly stitch (828 grey green)*
    - *—flame, antique bugle bead*
    - *—flower, outline, colonial knots (Cascade House cream)*
    - *—centre (Perle no. 5 light pink)*
    - *holly leaves, continuous fly stitch (828 grey green)*
    - *candy cane—outline, stem stitch (Cascade House cream)*
    - *—stripes, two rows of chain stitch (DMC Perle No 5 dark green)*
    - *Christmas tree—three triangles, continuous fly stitch (828 grey green)*

—*trunk, three satin stitches (828 grey green)*
• *gift box—outline of box, stem stitch (Cascade House cream)*
—*wrapping ribbon, three rows of stem stitch (Perle no. 5 light pink)*

MAKE THE RIBBONS

3. To make the ribbon bow on the candy stick: make five loops with two tails of ⅝" (15 mm) long each. From an ⅛" x 4" (3 mm x 10 cm) piece, make one loop of ⁹⁄₁₆" (14 mm) with two tails. Sew the two bows together—through the bit where the loops meet—to the candy stick, using ecru thread and colonial knots.

4. To make the ribbon flower on the candle: fold the silk ribbon in half, lengthwise. Sew running stitches along the pink edge. Gather up the ribbon to the desired size and attach it in place over the flower on the design. Sew a pearl bead into the centre.

5. To make the ribbon bow on the gift box: make four loops and two tails. Hold the ribbon in place with a centre pearl surrounded by five Mill Hill gold beads.

ATTACH THE EXTRAS

6. Make each candles for the tree by sewing on a gold bead and an antique bugle bead together.

7. Make the flame for the candle using a bugle bead.

8. Sew on the remaining eight pearl beads for holly berries.

9. Attach the brass star to the top of the Christmas tree.

FINISHING THE BANNER

10. See Techniques for how to quilt (page 16).

11. Quilt along the outside of each shaded brown edge bordering the snowflake section, the centre boxes and between the double edges of the boxes where they meet the letter boxes.

12. Finish the banner (see Techniques), and attach the brass Christmas tree to the bottom centre point.

13. Hang the banner (see Techniques).

Baby Bag

COLOUR ON CREAM

actual size

Materials

Homespun: 8½" x 7½" (21 cm x 19 cm).

Baby fabric of choice: 38" x 36" (97 cm x 92 cm).

Wadding: 38" x 36" (97 cm x 92 cm).

Lining fabric: 38" x 36" (97 cm x 92 cm).

Pockets in lining fabric: 12½" x 12" (33 cm x 31 cm); and 12" x 6½" (31 cm x 16.5 cm).

Handles in baby fabric: 9' 6" x 5" (2.88 m x 13 cm).

Terry towelling in a matching colour: 37" x 17" (94 cm x 43 cm)—or a purchased towel.

Threads

DMC Perle no. 5 (blue).

DMC Perle no. 8 (225 pink), (715 blue), (92 shaded green) and (ecru).

Cascade House Australia (yellow).

Extras

Velcro: 6" x 1" (15 cm x 2.5 cm).

Satin ribbon to match fabric: 36" x ½" (92 cm x 1.5 cm) for edging the towel motif.

Procedure

EMBROIDER THE MOTIF

1. Transfer the Hearts for Baby design onto the 8 ½" x 7 ½" (21 cm x 19 cm) piece of homespun (see Techniques).

2. Stitch the design as follows:
    • *letters—outline, stem stitch (no. 5, blue)*
    —fill, colonial knots (yellow)
    • *flowers—large, continuous fly stitch (225 pink)*
    —small, detached chain stitch (225 pink)

1. Cut out paper pattern following black lines and measurements

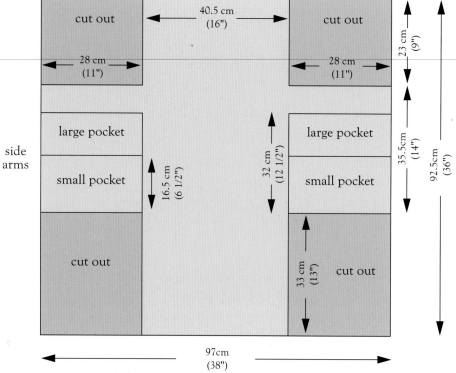

Top

| cut out | 40.5 cm (16") | cut out |

28 cm (11")

28 cm (11")

23 cm (9")

large pocket

large pocket

small pocket

32 cm (12 1/2")

small pocket

35.5cm (14")

92.5cm (36")

side arms

16.5 cm (6 1/2")

cut out

33 cm (13")

cut out

97cm (38")

2. To fold bag closed

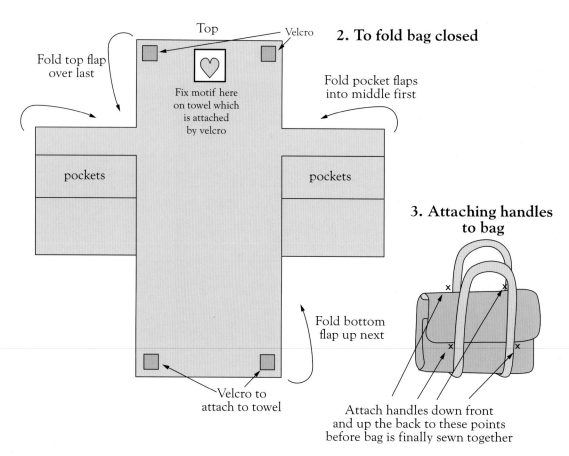

Top

Velcro

Fold top flap over last

Fold pocket flaps into middle first

Fix motif here on towel which is attached by velcro

pockets

pockets

3. Attaching handles to bag

Fold bottom flap up next

Velcro to attach to towel

Attach handles down front and up the back to these points before bag is finally sewn together

- *centres, colonial knots (ecru)*
- *tendrils, stem stitch (92 shaded green)*
- *heart, colonial knots (yellow)*
  —outline, stem stitch (no. 5, blue)
- *leaves, detached chain stitch (92 shaded green)*
- *dots on ribbon loops, colonial knots (ecru).*

MAKE THE HANDLES

3. Sew the baby fabric—right sides together—into a long cylinder. Turn the cylinder right side out.

4. Hand sew the ends together to make one long circle. Position the handles on the bag, as shown in picture (3). Pin along both sides of the handles, then machine stitch the handles firmly to the fabric—all the way along to the points indicated in the drawing.

ASSEMBLE THE BAG

5. Make a paper pattern from the diagram (1) and cut out the baby fabric, lining and wadding (note the top of the pattern). If your fabric has a one-way design, make sure the paper pattern is positioned to suit the design.

6. Cut the pockets. Fold them in half, lengthways. Sew them—on three sides—to the side 'arms' of the lining, making sure the inside edges are turned under to leave a neat finish.

7. Layer the pieces as follows:
   - *wadding*
   - *lining with pockets, right side up*
   - *baby fabric (handles folded away from the seams), wrong side up.*

8. Overlock (or zigzag) all around the edge, leaving a gap on one of the side 'arms'.

9. Pull the bag through the gap, and hand stitch the gap in the seam.

10. Press the edges lightly.

11. To strengthen the edges of the bag, sew a row of stitching ½" (1 cm) in from the edges.

MAKE UP THE TOWEL

12. Cut the purchased towel to size, overlock (or zigzag) the edge and turn under a single ½" (1 cm) hem.

13. If you haven't purchased a towel, make one up by turning a double hem of ½" (1 cm) on all the edges of the terry towelling, and machine stitching it in place.

14. Zigzag the embroidered motif to the top of the towel.

15. Lay the satin ribbon over the zigzag stitching around the edges of the motif, and stitch the ribbon in place.

16. Cut the velcro into four 1½" (4 cm) pieces.

17. Attach the velcro to each corner of the towel using a strong thread like quilting cotton. Put the two soft pieces at the top corners and two rough pieces at the bottom corners.

18. Attach the corresponding pieces—by hand—to the inside top and bottom corners of the bag. Be careful not to sew through to the outside of the bag.

Note: When washing the towel or the bag, fasten the corners together to prevent the velcro from catching in the wash.

STITCH GUIDE

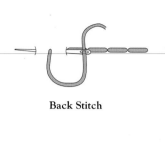

Back Stitch

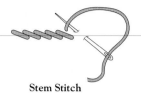

Stem Stitch

Whipped stem stitch

1   2   3   4

Bullion stitch

 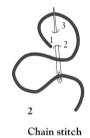 

1   2   3   **Buttonhole stitch**

Chain stitch

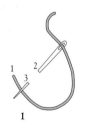   

1   2   3   1   2

Fly stitch

**Detached chain stitch
(Lazy Daisy Stitch)**

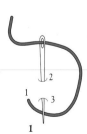 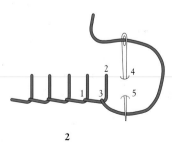

1   2

Blanket stitch

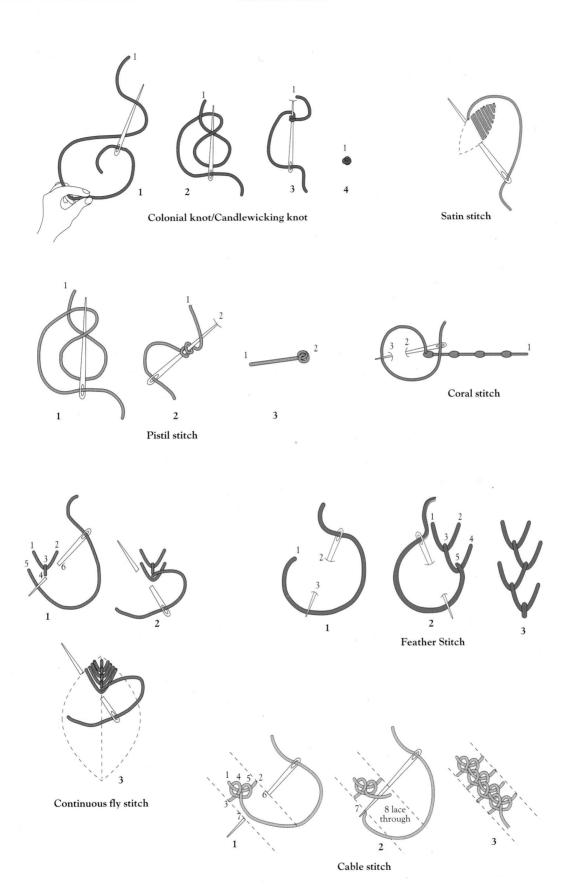

Colonial knot/Candlewicking knot

Satin stitch

Pistil stitch

Coral stitch

Feather Stitch

Continuous fly stitch

8 lace
through

Cable stitch

SUPPLIERS

EDMAR RAYON THREADS
Plain, shaded and variegated

EdMar
PO Box 55
Camarillo CA 93010-0055
USA
E-mail: edmar@edmar-co.com
Online catalogue: www.edmar-co.com

Ristal Threads
PO Box 134
Mitchell ACT 2911
AUSTRALIA
Phone: 61 (02) 6241 2293

PERLE THREADS NO. 5, 8, 12
Variegated and shaded

Minnamurra Threads
PO Box 374
Glebe NSW 2037
AUSTRALIA
Phone / Fax: 61 (02) 9570 7004

CANDLEWICKING COTTON
Nine country shades including cream and white

Cascade House Australia
PO Box 4054
Langwarrin VIC 3910
AUSTRALIA
Email: cascade@cascadeyarns.com.au
Online catalogue:
www.cascadeyarns.com.au

CERAMIC BUTTONS
Handcrafted, full gloss or terracotta, kiln fired

Annie Lane Designs
PO Box 824
Muswellbrook NSW 2333
AUSTRALIA
Phone: 61 0419 274 263
E-mail:
annielanedesigns@bigpond.com

SPECIALIST MACHINE QUILTING
Jenny Eisner
Charm Cottage Quilts & Collectables
13 Norah Ave
Charmhaven NSW 2263
AUSTRALIA
Phone: 61 (02) 4392 8396